Roy Kane TV Detective

Steve Bowkett

Illustrated by David Burroughs

A & C Black · London

GRAFFIX

Roller Madonnas · Bernard Ashley
Roy Kane TV Detective · Steve Bowkett
Bodyparts · Theresa Breslin
Moving the Goalposts · Rob Childs
Captain Hawk · Jim Eldridge
Laser Quest · Mick Gowar
Matthew's Goals · Michael Hardcastle
Thirteen Candles · Mary Hooper
The Headless Ghost · Pete Johnson
The Listener · Elizabeth Laird
A Boy Like That · Tony Langham
Biker · Anthony Masters
Otherworld · Jeremy Strong
Lovesick · Lynda Waterhouse

First paperback edition 1999
First published 1998 in hardback by
A & C Black (Publishers) Ltd
35 Bedford Row, London WC1R 4JH

Text copyright © 1998 Steve Bowkett
Illustrations copyright © 1998 David Burroughs
Cover illustration copyright © 1998 Peter Dennis

The right of Steve Bowkett to be identified as author
of this work has been asserted by him in accordance
with the Copyrights, Designs and Patents Act 1988.

ISBN 0-7136-4955-0

A CIP catalogue for this book is available from
the British Library.

Printed and bound in Spain by G. Z. Printek, Bilbao.

Chapter One

Thursday, October 14th, 6.42 p.m.
Clayton City Museum had been closed since 5.00 p.m.
The only person in the building was Alistair Harvey,
the Museum Director...

Suddenly the alarm triggered...

EEEEEEEE

Sergeant Greg Mulholland and Officer Brad Michalik were first on the scene, where they found a distraught Alistair Harvey pacing up and down.

The three men walked through shadowy corridors and galleries until they reached a new exhibition.

THE MAGIC OF ANCIENT EGYPT

Harvey strode quickly past the exhibits, leading the police officers to a large, glittering - and empty - showcase.

9

CCTV Studios, 7.05 p.m.
Mulholland and Michalik had arranged to meet Roy Kane at the TV studio. They arrived just as Roy was finishing his latest episode of 'Kane On The Case'.

...And so that's how the case was solved. Who would have believed that a humble scientist would have used his latest invention, an all-purpose glue, to turn to a life of crime?

But one thing's for sure - Dario Menzel, 'The Human Spider', came unstuck in the end. This is Roy Kane wishing you well until the next episode of 'Kane On The Case'. Thank you and goodnight!

Mulholland explained about the robbery at the Museum.

'So you're telling me the alarm went off after the diamond was taken?' Roy said, frowning. 'And there was no forced entry... Have you checked the security camera video?'

Mulholland shrugged heavily. 'Not yet.'

'Leave that to me,' said Roy. He took out a notepad and scribbled an address.

Jez Mackintosh's house, 8.54 p.m.
Jez had used his skills to help Roy on a number of
past cases. But could he help him now? Roy's other
assistant, Vicki Stand, was also there. They listened
as Roy filled them in on the details of the robbery.

...So no-one saw an intruder
enter or leave?

There's nothing captured
on the security videos.

What about the footage
from the Jewel Room itself -
have you scanned that yet?

Took a quick look just
before Vicki turned up.
Check this out...

Jez pushed a button and a picture of the Egyptian Jewel Room glowed on a nearby screen.

Now look... there... just for a few seconds, a strange mist obscures the Kay-To-Bah Diamond.

When the mist fades, the jewel has gone.

Yes, but that doesn't help us.

It might do. I can process the footage to filter out the fog...

Jez worked at the keyboard for a few minutes.

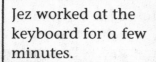

Okay, let's run it again.

A second later...

EEEEEEEEEEEE

Well, at least we know it wasn't aliens from outer space!

But it's pretty advanced trickery all the same. I think we need some technical advice.

There's a magician playing at the Deangate Theatre - Doctor Praetorius. Maybe he can help us.

Good idea. Jez, will you carry on working with this security video? Vicki and I will go and see if this 'Doctor Praetorius' is all he's cracked up to be...

Chapter Two

I think Doctor Praetorius is still in his dressing room. Follow me.

I've seen Praetorius on the TV. Some of the things he does are amazing!

Clever trickery actually, Vicki. That's all...

MR ALBERT WATTS
DR. PRAETORIUS

KNOCK!

Come in.

15

Roy and Vicki stepped inside. The room was an Aladdin's cave of treasures filled with the props and equipment Praetorius used to perform his mind-boggling illusions. The magician, and his wife and assistant, Lisa, were busy tidying up after the show.

Roy explained about the missing Kay-To-Bah Diamond, and the trickery that had seemingly been used to steal it.

'I'm sorry, Mr Kane,' Praetorius said when Roy had finished. 'But I can't help you.'

Roy and Vicki drove back across town to see how Jez had been getting on...

Well, even if he couldn't help us, I still think his magic is amazing...

Call it detective's intuition, but I thought there was more to Praetorius than meets the eye.

Surely you'd expect one of the world's greatest magicians to be a little mysterious?

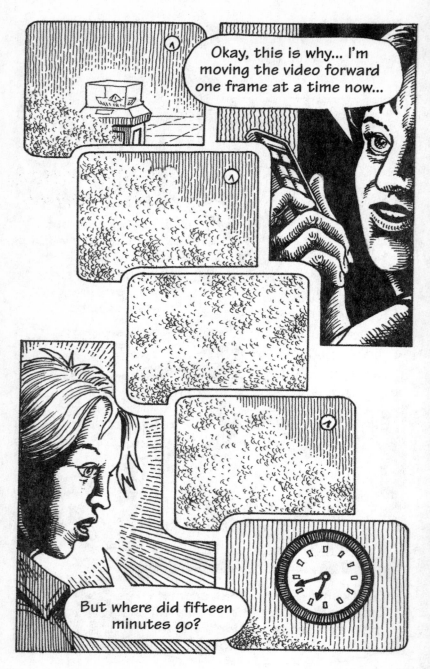

Saturday, October 16th, 11.25 p.m.
At a downtown warehouse a security guard carried out his routine checks. A shadowy figure watched from a distance.

Suddenly the building was engulfed in flames.

Emergency services were quickly on the scene. Roy and his team arrived soon afterwards.

What's the situation?

We've got the blaze under control now, but the contents of the warehouse have been completely destroyed. There's not much doubt this was done deliberately.

We've found an empty petrol can and traces of the incendiary device that started the fire. I've got men up on the roof - someone was spotted up there, before the fire started.

Any chance we could take a look up there, Chief?

Sure, just follow me.

Roy launched himself at the shadowy figure...

WHUMP!

...but the cape was empty.

Super-lightweight compressible plastic. It's just another trick, Roy. But it's the same caped figure that we saw on the Museum video.

Let's get back to the car, I want to check something on the computer.

29

31

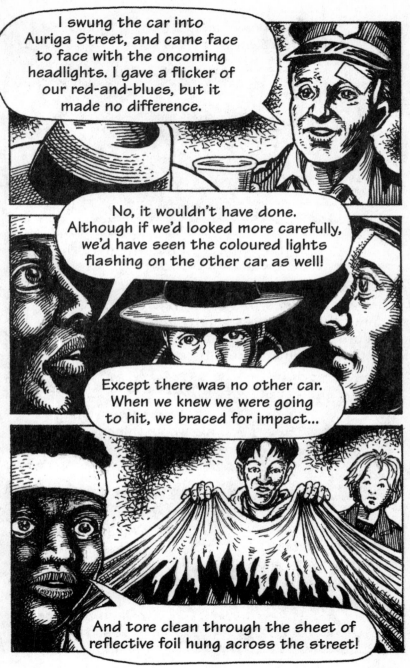

It was pure bad luck that the front offside wheel hit the kerb.

'Bad luck nothing,' Mulholland grumbled.

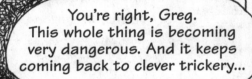

If you ask me this stunt was carefully arranged. The caped figure prepared that foil sheet beforehand, to fool us. By ducking down that alley, he lured us into Auriga Street...

You're right, Greg. This whole thing is becoming very dangerous. And it keeps coming back to clever trickery...

So do we grill Doctor Praetorius again?

All in good time. First I want to meet the other player in the game - Magnus Carmody. We'll go and see him first thing on Monday morning...

Half an hour later, they pulled up outside a large portacabin. Huge skeletal structures towered upwards all around them. Roy knocked at the door and they went inside.

Hello. I'm Roy Kane, and this is my colleague, Vicki Stand. We have an appointment with -

I'm Magnus Carmody. What can I do for you?

Roy ran through the details that had brought them to see Carmody; the theft of the Kay-To-Bah Diamond, and the arson attack on Carmody's warehouse.

So how can I help? You're the detective!

Some information would be helpful. For instance, do you know of anyone who has a grudge against you?

41

Right, let's get backstage and have a snoop around. No need to talk to anyone, just see if you can pick up some gossip, any details that might help us.

Roy walked round the back of the theatre to the stage door and mingled with the fans waiting to catch a glimpse of Doctor Praetorius. Meanwhile, Vicki made her way towards the dressing rooms. There was a heated argument going on.

But it isn't my fault if audience figures are dropping! My act is the best there is - I'm Doctor Praetorius!

The door slammed shut and Vicki ducked behind a curtain as the Theatre Manager stormed by. When he'd gone, she turned to sneak away but there, standing right in front of her, was Doctor Praetorius...

Chapter Four

Ohhh - what happened?

But - how? You're in two places at once!

What's going on?

Roy... Praetorius... he...

I seem to have startled your young assistant. She fainted when she saw me.

There's really nothing to be frightened of.

It's a trick we often use in our act. I 'disappear', then miraculously reappear elsewhere - but of course it's Lisa in disguise.

May I?

This mask is made of ultrafine rubber and it looks exactly like skin. Simple, but brilliant, Mr Watts.

That's Lisa's expertise.

I studied Art and Design at university, specialising in human portraiture.

She could have made a name for herself as a sculptress - but married me instead and devoted her life to our act.

45

Well it fooled me!

The mask is a trade secret. Albert and I would not want you to reveal it to anyone.

We won't do anything to ruin the illusion, Mrs Watts. Not if we can help it...

A short while later, in Roy's car.

Do you still suspect that Praetorius is the Shadowman?

I'm keeping my options open, but the evidence is stacked against him.

47

Pen Flats Site Office, 10.27 p.m.
The site was deserted, except for Magnus Carmody,
who had been working late.

As Carmody reached his car the darkness was
pierced by a brilliant beam of light and a huge
shadow appeared.

49

Carmody ran to his car. He revved the engine and sped away.

SCREEE

A traffic patrol unit was parked on the highway watching for speeding motorists.

VROOOM!

Looks like he's in a hurry. Let's get after him.

AAAAWWEEEEE

Jez stepped back and flipped a switch. A cloud of mist instantly rose up around him - and out of the mist loomed the Grim Reaper himself.

What we have here is a holographic projector, coupled with a gas cylinder which produces the mist. It's brilliant.

CLICK!

So, someone planted this device in Carmody's car, either to scare the living daylights out of him, or to kill him.

Another fancy illusion. I think it's time Albert Watts was pulled in for questioning. I'll ring Chief Inspector Lane and arrange it...

And it nearly succeeded.

A few seconds later Mr Watts appeared.

Sir, we simply need to ask about your where-abouts tonight, and one or two other matters. It's just routine.

I don't understand - my wife says you want to question me? Why?

I was about to turn in for the night. Really, this is most unusual...

What the...

Chapter Five

Well, how can I ever thank you? This is simply wonderful! Did you catch the thief, by the way?

Yes, we -

The evidence is circumstantial, Mr Harvey. We're still investigating the case.

Well, this beautiful diamond has been returned, and that's all that matters...

A few minutes later.

Come on, Greg. You told me about the look on Watts' face - he was as surprised as the rest of you. The jewel could easily have been planted.

What do you mean 'the evidence is circumstantial'! Watts was caught red-handed, with the diamond.

Besides, you've been questioning Watts all night, and has he admitted it yet?

No chance. He's pleading ignorance.

Well maybe he's telling the truth. Let's wait and see...

57

A short time later, Roy and Vicki arrived at Jez's apartment.

What's the news on Carmody then, Vicki?

Well, Watts and Carmody not only attended the same High School, they also studied at Clayton University. And, it was there they met Lisa Harrison, later to become Mrs Watts.

So?

So the grudge between Watts and Carmody grew worse. They were both interested in Lisa. She married Watts and they moved away. Carmody started up his business and grew rich...

And now Watts and Lisa have returned to Clayton, bought a home here and intend to settle.

Carmody is being tormented all over again...

Okay, here's another connection.

You asked me to cross-check Carmody's companies with ticket sales at the theatres where 'Dr Praetorius' has been appearing...

Praetorius' audiences have been small...

But the figures say ticket sales are good.

The Deangate Theatre, 9.12 a.m.

Mr Watson, do you have a moment?

What do you want?

61

Sir, we want to talk to you about the block-buying of tickets...

I don't know anything...

And I also wonder if you 'don't know anything' about a rather expensive diamond, Mr Watson?

I - I -

Did Magnus Carmody pay you to plant that diamond in Albert Watts' coat pocket?

No, that wasn't me! I had nothing to do with that.

After him.

Let's see how he likes this!

THUD!

Roy took out his phone and keyed in a number. A moment later the voice of Magnus Carmody's secretary answered.

I'll put you through.

Oh, hello. I'd like to speak with Mr Carmody please, it's quite urgent.

Carmody here –

CLICK!

So, Carmody isn't the Shadowman, it seems...

Then who is?

Just at this moment, Vicki, your guess is as good as mine.

Chapter Six

Tuesday, October 19th, 11.26 a.m.
Roy and Vicki met up with Jez in a cafe not far from the Deangate Theatre.

The Shadowman would have killed you, Roy...

He knows we're getting close. And since the trap was sprung at the theatre, the Deangate and the Shadowman must be connected.

Well we know the Shadowman's not Albert Watts, he's still in custody...

And we know the Shadowman isn't Carmody. He was at work.

So, if we rule out Carmody, that leaves somebody we don't know about yet... or Lisa Watts.

What!

Okay, okay, it's just an idea.

But we're playing a dangerous game now, so we can't afford to miss a single trick. If we assume that the Shadowman intends to destroy Carmody, his Head Office is likely to be the next target.

Do we stake it out?

We don't know when the Shadowman will next strike. I've got another plan...

1.19 p.m. Stage 1 of the plan. Roy dropped Vicki outside the Watts' house.

Oh, Miss Stand. What do you want?

We have reason to believe that the Shadowman may be planning to harm you. I've been asked to stay with you for your protection.

But...

So with Lisa Watts covered, if the Shadowman shows up we'll know she's in the clear.

Clever.

Okay, let's get over to Carmody's office block.

1.45 p.m. Stage 2 of the plan: Carmody's office. Roy explained to the security guard at Reception that he had police authorisation to check the building's surveillance system, on the suspicion that the Shadowman may have targeted Magnus Carmody.

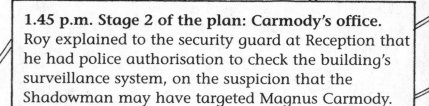

Is Mr Carmody in the building right now?

No sir, but he's expected later.

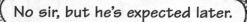

Okay, we'll speak with him then. Come on Jez...

By the way, did you sort out the phone tap?

Yes. If anyone phones Carmody's office, we'll pick it up on the tap, which is patched through to the mobile.

Lisa checked that Vicki was unconscious, before hurrying from the house.

Back in Roy's car, Jez continued to monitor the security cameras on his computer. All was normal but suddenly the building's cameras blanked out. Jez checked his cameras - they were still working. One of them showed a strange mist billowing into the lobby. The security guard was unconscious.

Check this out, Roy!

The guard's out cold. The Shadowman must be going for Carmody!

Better warn him.

Just as Roy took out his phone, it began to ring. Jez watched the computer screen and saw Carmody pick up his phone, too.

BRR BRR

BRR BRR

Darling, it's me. Albert's been released. I'm coming for you now...

I'M COMING FOR YOU NOW!

The Shadowman's voice!

I'm calling Vicki.

It was several minutes before Vicki answered her phone.

I don't know what happened, Roy, but Lisa Watts has vanished!

...Okay Vicki, come over here now. We're going up to Carmody's office.

Chapter Seven

Roy and Jez hurried to the lobby of the building. They checked that the guard was all right, before taking the elevator to Carmody's private office. In the outer office they found his secretary unconscious. Once inside Carmody's room, they discovered signs of a struggle.

Roy's phone rang. It was Mulholland, telling Roy that Albert Watts had given them the slip.

And he's sure to be heading this way - because even if Watts isn't the Shadowman, he knows who he is.

Carmody reached the edge of the roof and peered down. Far below, police cars screeched to a halt and officers rushed into the building. Carmody turned to retrace his steps.

Now, Carmody - now you pay. After all these years of hate, I have you.

You ridiculed me. You tried to destroy my career. You even took my wife away from me.

Don't you think poor stupid Albert Watts could be the mysterious Shadowman?

But... but I don't understand. What have I ever done to you?

Watts? It can't be you...

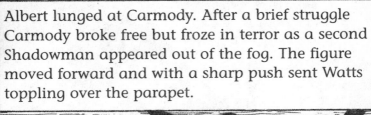

Albert lunged at Carmody. After a brief struggle Carmody broke free but froze in terror as a second Shadowman appeared out of the fog. The figure moved forward and with a sharp push sent Watts toppling over the parapet.

Aargh!

Fearing for his life, Carmody stumbled away, but not quickly enough. The second Shadowman pulled a gun and fired once... twice. The bullet caught Carmody's leg and he crashed to the ground. The Shadowman moved in for the kill.

BLAM!

BLAM!

Suddenly Roy appeared out of the shadows.

Lisa, I think that's enough, don't you?

After all they did? After all the empty promises.

He just wanted me to be another of his possessions.

But what about Albert? Surely you loved him?

I envied his brilliance, but I came to loathe him for being nothing more than a stage magician - and me, his obedient little assistant. We could have done so much!

79